M3

Media Marketing Method

By Ryan Stewman

M3

Media Marketing Method

ISBN: 9781729308967

Cover design by Sooraj Mathew

HARDCORE RESOURCES

SOCIAL MEDIA

Facebook

286,000 followers

Fan: www.facebook.com/hardcorecloser

Sales Talk With Sales Pros Group:

www.facebook.com/groups/salestalk

Personal: www.facebook.com/realryanstewman

Twitter

16,300 followers

Personal: www.twitter.com/ryanstewman

Business: www.twitter.com/hardcorecloser

LinkedIn

12,400 followers

Personal: www.linkedin.com/in/ryanstewman

Business:

www.linkedin.com/company/hardcorecloser

Instagram

119,000 followers

Personal: www.instagram.com/ryanstewman

Business: www.instagram.com/hardcorecloser

YouTube

3.5 million views/10M minutes watched

www.youtube.com/user/ryanstewman

Snapchat

ryanstewman

Skype

ryanstewman

<u>PODCASTS</u>

THC Podcast

Top 50 Business Podcast on iTunes, 60K listeners

Get Your Mind Right Podcast

Top 50 Business Podcast on iTunes, 60K listeners

BESTSELLING BOOKS

- *Social Media Millions: Your Guide to Making Massive Amounts of Money from Social Media Selling*

- *Sell It and Scale It: How to Transition from Salesman to CEO* (2017)

- *F*ck Your Excuses: The Misfit's Guide to Avoiding Upper Limits* (2017)

- *Elevator to the Top: Your Go-To Resource for All Things Sales* (2016)

- *Bulletproof Business: Protect Yourself Against the Competition* (2016)

- *Kick Ass - Take Names, Emails and Phone Numbers* (2015)
- *Hardcore [c]loser*, A Top Business Book of all Time, Amazon (2015)

WEBSITES

Hardcore Closer Blog

500,000 Visitors Monthly

www.HardcoreCloser.com

Articles, Digital Products, Training Resources

Break Free Academy

www.BreakFreeAcademy.com

Funnel Closers

www.FunnelClosers.com

Phone Sites

www.PhoneSites.com

Clyxo

www.Clyxo.com/Closer

Table of Contents

Chapter 1: EdgeRank

Before we get started you need to know that I can help you reach your social media goals no matter the industry you're in.

I've helped people in the jewelry business. I've helped people in the mortgage business. I've helped people in real estate, and I have helped a lot of coaches and small business owners, too. What I am about to share with you in this book works in any industry or field.

My biggest talent on this planet is not social media marketing; it's not knowing sales strategies. It's not advertising. My biggest talent is actually taking really complex stuff and making it simple to understand.

Dumb asses don't read books like this. They don't go to seminars. They don't buy programs. They don't watch videos. That's the difference between dumb people and smart people. Smart folks are not on social media checking out Kim Kardashian pictures, but they are on social media trying to figure out how to grow their business. They go there to market and network with people. And there is one other thing about smart people that you should know. They have a tendency to take very simple stuff and complicate it.

Because you are reading this book, I know you're smart.

So, as a smart person, two thoughts will go through your mind: number one, you might think *well that's not going to work for my business*. Number two is: *it can't be that simple*.

I am sharing the information in this book to debunk both of those myths. It can work for you, and it is simple, easy-to-learn, and even easier to implement.

I've learned through my career as a salesperson, business owner and comedian that the simpler something is, the easier it is for the person on the other end to make a decision. When you complicate things, people have a hard time making a decision because you're giving them too much information to process.

That's why a lot of times people will say, "I need to think about it." What they really mean is that they need to figure out what it is that you sold them. You've given them too much to think about. Keeping things simple is how you make money in sales. I am going to take a lot of big complicated strategies and break them down, so you can follow them quickly and easily, which means you can also duplicate what I'm telling you to experience your own success.

I'm going to let you in on the same tactics I've used to persuade people to purchase an event from me, so you can use them with your audience and persuade them to purchase your products and services.

As you read this book, I just ask that you don't overcomplicate what I will share with you. Don't tell yourself those two lies I mentioned. That it won't work for you and it can't be that simple. That is a sign that your brain has been hit by the force of average. Be open to the knowledge I'm about to drop and after you read this book, make sure you put what you've learned into practice. The majority of people won't follow through. Make sure you are not one of them. After all, why did you pick up this book?

The key to reaching the success that you want is to actually go out and do it. You're going to make some mistakes. I tell my new sales staff all the time that it's okay to be on the phone with a client and tell them you don't know the answer to a question or to make a mistake. Don't let the fear of making a mistake hold you back from using what you read in this book. Remember this phrase: imperfect action. Then do it.

When you get started, keep going because if you wait until everything's perfect, it'll never happen. Again, I have seen good intentions go bad too many times. A reader gets all jacked up and wanting to get started on what they learned, but then they get afraid and return to their comfort zone. I already know you're going to make a few posts on social media and maybe your mother or your sister or an ex-business partner or your secretary will go "Who the hell do you think you are? Tai Lopez? You're just going to post all the time now? Are you trying to be like Joe Rogan? You think you're Kim Kardashian? What's going on here?"

When that happens, it means you are living the real-life theory of crabs in a bucket.

Let me explain.

When you throw a bunch of crabs in a bucket if one of them climbs across the rest of them and almost makes its way out of the bucket the ones on the bottom will pull it back down to be back with the rest of the crab gang. People do that, too. This happens as you stand out more online, as you stand out more in business. There will be people who try to force you back into the box of their comfort zone. You might call them haters, or some other name. But I'm calling them crabs.

Don't listen to these people when they pop up and talk negatively to you. All I ask is that you keep taking action. Every day, I make posts, and people tell me I have fucked-up hair. As if I didn't know I was born with 10 cowlicks. Of course, I already know that. People tell me I brag too much. But if I'd have let that stop me, you wouldn't be reading this book. I would have quit 10 years ago before I got where I'm at today. Stuff's going to happen to you, and that's the force of average trying to get you to go back to where you came from. But after you put this book down, you'll have to make the decision of whether or not you will turn over a new leaf.

If it'll work for me, it'll work for you. I'm an extreme case. Think about the story that I tell online. Prison, drugs, adoption, quitting school. A lot of people may have some of that in their background, but most people won't have all of those events.

Whatever it is that's happened in your past; whatever it is that happens in the future, it doesn't matter. It's not going to hold you back today. Make a decision that you're going to step outside of your comfort zone and make big moves. We live in a world that's easily connected from our fingertips on a phone. There are two billion+ people we can connect with immediately, and if you know how to use the algorithm and what I am going to teach you, then you can get in touch with anybody anyplace, anytime, anywhere. But if you don't utilize these tools correctly, if you go back to your comfort zone, you'll never get what you want in life.

A lot of us think we don't deserve good things in life. Consider the number of people who have had an outstanding month. Maybe they made a bunch of money, only to be followed by a really shitty month because they took their foot off the gas. Or they took their foot off the gas because they got lazy. Once you start this process in social media, you have to continue it. If I go two or three days without posting guess what happens on my page? I lose all the credibility that I have. I'll use lose all the momentum. People will go to my page one or two days in a row, and they'll think: *I guess Ryan's not posting anymore.* When that happens, then you're obsolete again.

What happens when you don't see your friends? Let's talk about your mother for example. She's usually the person we love the most. If we don't see her post on social media for a couple of days, we don't even think about her. That's because we're only thinking about what's in our newsfeed. So, we've got to do our best to make sure that we're in everybody's newsfeed. That means constantly taking action and doing exactly what I am teaching you in this book.

We know if a person is ranked number one in using SEO keywords it's because they've consistently put in the backlinks. They've consistently tied in the keywords. But still, it's a work in progress, and it takes time to build up to that top status. Building up your social media happens in the same way.

Before we cover the specifics that you need to know on social media, first, I want to cue you in on how the algorithm works. Then you can apply that knowledge for your own benefit.

Every social media site uses a universal algorithm. It doesn't matter whether you're using Snapchat, Instagram, Facebook or LinkedIn. This algorithm applies to all of these applications.

In my business and personal life, I use Instagram and Facebook the most. I'm on all the other sites, and I occasionally post there (other than Snapchat). I just don't get that app, and so I don't mess around. Also, that's not where my audience is, so I don't focus on it. And you always want to be where your audience is.

Last month alone, we made over $50,000 in sales from Instagram, so right now Instagram's my main focus. Of course, that's only one revenue channel, and obviously, we still do a lot more on Facebook, but I'm seeing the shift happen. More and more people are into Instagram and Instagram is owned by Facebook. So, when I talk about the Facebook algorithm, remember, this applies to Instagram also. Since these are the main platforms, this is where I am concentrating the focus.

Last month, we made $353,000 from Facebook for Break Free Academy. How we made that money all boils down to what is called EdgeRank.

There are three parts to EdgeRank, which is the algorithm of how Facebook works. Maybe you have heard that EdgeRank went away in 2014. Maybe some modern social media guru will argue with you that it's gone, but remember, methods are many, and principles are few. Methods may vary, but principles never do. Just because Prince changed his name into a symbol, doesn't mean he wasn't still in existence. This is exactly the case with EdgeRank.

Facebook's changed the name of EdgeRank into a symbol, but the truth is EdgeRank was there at the start of Facebook; it is still there, and it is the foundation.

EdgeRank is powerful. Supposedly, it's won elections. Supposedly, it's changed public opinion and the way that people present the news to us. It's the reason we get to decide if we want to see Gary Vee every other scroll in our newsfeed versus people that we actually want to hear from like our friends and family. That's all based on the algorithm called EdgeRank. Once you master what works and you learn how to use it to your own benefit, yours will be the post people will see all the time.

As I say often: "People buy from people they know, like and trust." But for people to make that decision of whether they like you and trust you, they have to know who the hell you are. To know who the hell you are, they have to see your content on a regular basis. I'm not ignorant to the fact that a person goes through phases each time they see me online. If they've never seen me and if we're advertising to cold traffic they're probably thinking *who is this guy?*

But the next time, they might see my video again and think *hmmm, here he is again. I might as well check and see what he's doing—I mean this thing's not gonna stop appearing in my newsfeed.*

So, then they'll watch a video for a couple of minutes. And they might think it's cool A couple of days later when they see me again, I'll get a little bit more from them. Then, they can ultimately make the decision that *this guy knows what he's talking about.*

This is how they eventually buy from me. When you start to get in front of prospects in your newsfeed, the familiarity breeds them into making that decision of whether they know, like and trust you. Once they know you, only then can they make the decision to move forward with you.

There are three components to EdgeRank. None are more important than the other. Part one is called weight. Without one, you can't have the others. You have to have all the parts in motion for this system to work well for you.

Weight equals the amount of likes, comments, shares and replies, etc. on a post. In essence, this is the way people engage with your post.

I post a lot of links to blog sites and HardcoreCloser.com. I've written over 1,100 blog posts at this point in time. So, for me, it's really easy to grab four or five blog posts from HardcoreCloser.com in the morning and share them to all my groups.

People click on them and read them. They like the posts.

Let's say a person makes a comment on my post, and then 15-20 other people reply; that adds weight. I also get weight from the invisible actions people take—like tagging someone, etc.

Weight is all about engagement and so the more engagement you have on your posts, the heavier the weight. There's another invisible way that people create weight. That's by copying the URL and sending it to somebody through messenger or in an email. You don't see that the person has done that. But when they do, it contributes to the weight.

For example, I'll copy the link and go into one of my groups like Entourage, Funnel Closer or Push to Excellence.

My post will let people know the link is in the first comment because not as many people will get to see your post when you put the link right in the post. It will say "If you guys would leave comments and testimonials, so people will know that this is the real deal and be influenced to buy, I'd appreciate it." When people click the link and interact, even though the link is in the comment, you still get that weight credit.

You can't create your own weight, but we see people try to do that. If you leave 15 comments on your own post, it doesn't help because you can't add to your own weight. You have to have other people's likes and engagement. If you are the only person engaging on your post, you will stay the only person engaging on your post.

Facebook gets paid by the amount of time the user spends online. The longer a person spends on Facebook, the better.

But how do you get people to engage with you? The easiest way is to ask a question.

You want to do this because what really elicits weight and engagement on a page is engaging your audience. Post about trends and controversy, etc. Make sure that you whatever you talk about will intrigue people.

Some actions weigh more than others and therefore, impact your EdgeRank score more. For example, when someone likes a post that creates the least amount of weight possible.

So, if everybody's just hitting the like button, the weight will be low. If you leave a two-word reply, that's not a whole lot of weight either. But if you write a whole damn paragraph as a reply on somebody's post or somebody writes a paragraph reply on your post, Facebook goes *wow! This is engaging enough for this person to spend five minutes typing out their response.*

Facebook cares how long you spend in their little white box so the longer you type in there, the more weight that is added to your post. It sounds crazy, but if you make a one-sentence post on Facebook, and the box is only open for 30 seconds, it does not create as much weight on your post as it would if you were to write a whole paragraph that took you three or four minutes. Just for the record; if you type a post out and then delete it, just know Facebook has it stored in on their server. So, if any of you run for president in the future, they will bring up whatever you have written against you. Facebook stores everything.

After the likes, the next action that creates the most weight are the emojis, then comes shares, replies and finally saves.

I usually write posts that are three or four paragraphs long because I know after two paragraphs if you want to finish reading you've got to click "see more." Clicking the "see more" button adds invisible weight, too.

Using the "see more" trick is a cheap way to get people engaged, and for you to get some more weight out of your post. But if you click "see more," on a post that has 20 comments and you comment on number 19, for example, then you'll get more weight, too. The reason is that FB knows you not only spent all the time reading the comments, but you also get points because you clicked on the replies.

When you're making your post think about how you can get maximum effort out of the people who are participating. The more effort people exert, the heavier the weight.

The second component to EdgeRank is affinity. Affinity has to do with your connections. The human mind can only handle about 50 connections at a time, and Facebook stands on the faith that if you're connected to 5,000 people on your Facebook page, there's no way you can remember all of those people. There's no way that you give a shit about what all 5,000 of those people are doing. Instead, they try to pick out your top 50 people and keep them consistently going through your newsfeed.

But how would they decide that?

Facebook counts who you send DMs to and who you engage with and those are the people who will each see each other's content.

Thirty thousand people might see my posts, but I'm only seeing 50 people's posts. Your capacity to how many people can see you is unlimited, but you will be limited to the 50 people who you engage with the most in your newsfeed.

That said, you want to make sure you've got the right people looking at you. So, send people direct messages, and write on their wall. Birthdays don't count, by the way. Facebook zones out people's names when we first meet them as well. If I've got 50 wholesalers I want to do business with for my real estate business, I want to ensure every time I have a property for sale that they hit me up. So, I will do what I need to so the wholesalers will see what I want them to.

To do that, I will send them a DM, but I won't send them a DM telling them about the house for sale because that would get old quick.

Instead, I do what I call social reconnaissance. I'll go over to their wall and first like two or three of their posts. After that, I will send them a direct message like: "I was just on your wall and noticed that you'd been to the zoo with your family. I've been thinking about taking my family to the zoo. Was it really hot or were there air-conditioned places where you could actually hang out? Did you guys enjoy it?"

When you start a conversation with them, instead of going "Hey man, I've got this house for sale," give them a different sort of attention. They won't think *there's that guy, Stewman with his sales pitch.* No, they will think that it's pretty cool that someone is paying attention to them.

That's the whole reason people post on social media, so that people will pay attention to them. When you hit them up in the DM and ask them questions about their posts and life, that feels great.

This is the modern version of the old Dale Carnegie adage where he says, "If you want people to be interested in you, you have to be interested in them."

As it applies to social media, if you want people to be interested in you, then practice softer reconnaissance and send them a direct message. When you do that, you also garner affinity.

The second thing you want to do is, write on their wall. But you need to do this in a specific way. "I love seeing your posts. I just want you to know that you inspire me. You make me want to start a small business. I hope this encourages you to keep doing what you're doing." When the person reads your post, they will think *dude, that's awesome!*

It makes a person feel good when you write on their wall. The next thing you know, they are liking and engaging with you because they see your posts in their newsfeed.

The more you make social media about your audience and less about you, the more people will engage, because typically, everybody makes it about themselves. Doing the opposite sets you apart and makes you more appealing.

When I pay attention to everybody else, that person is appreciating me and thinking, *I really like Ryan because he's paying attention to me. I can't even get my wife to pay attention to me, or my kids or my boss to pay attention to me. My employees don't know I exist, but that Stewman? He pays attention to me.*

After all that happens, then the algorithm goes "these two people obviously like each other because they went out of the way to go to the wall and actually comment on a couple of their posts. I'll make sure that they start seeing each other in their newsfeeds."

If you think about it, when you get a direct message from somebody, all of a sudden, you'll start seeing them in your newsfeed all the time. This happens even if it's been six or seven months since you connected.

I always see my clients' and mentors' posts on FB, and that's about it. It makes sense because I'm constantly going to their pages. I want to make sure my clients are doing the work. I want to check out my mentors to see what they're doing to inspire people, and how I can possibly mimic it.

To recap, affinity refers to the people you're connected to. You will see about 50 people in your newsfeed, but that doesn't mean that only 50 people are going to see you.

I practice something called the Lucky 7 Method, which comprises three things and is about a month-long hustle. By the time it's over, you're so burned out that you have to take your foot off the gas.

Because it's so hard to consistently do this method for 90 days, much less 180 days—that's how successful it is. You will be drowning in leads and struggling to keep up—in the best way.

Here's what you need to do to get started with the Lucky 7 Method.

First, I write three posts on one person's wall.

Second, I DM one person.

Third, I comment on someone else's posts.

If you do that every day for 31 days, that's 93 engagements with 93 different people. That means FB will pick the 50 out for you and then that runs your reach to 93 people you've interacted with and created affinity with. The advantage is that most people don't have a bunch of people hitting them up in the DM. Most people don't have a bunch of people commenting and replying on their posts. Most people don't have writing on their walls so doing these things will bump you to the top of their list.

I recommend that you write down the top 25 to 50 people you'd like to do business with even if it's Tony Robbins, Grant Cardone or Tai Lopez. Make sure you give yourself a big audacious goal.

Start engaging on the posts of the people on your list. That's the only way you will get their attention.

Make sure that you're engaging with these people on a regular basis, too, and if you follow the Lucky 7 Method for 30 days and you write down 50 people, that's 50 more people than you started with.

Watch your time decay as you go through this method as well.

Time decay is the third component to EdgeRank, and it refers to the amount of time between when your post was publicized, and when the first comment was received. This is true even if your post has been up a while and someone comments on it. That starts the time decay clock all over again.

Once you make a post, you have about 60 seconds to get engagement. So, let's say that I've got 5,000 friends and 200 of them are online because obviously, not all 5,000 will be online at the same time. So, in this case, we'll imagine that when I make the post, 200 will be online. Facebook might show my post to 10 of those people. Out of those 10, five (or 50% of people) who were shown it, commented, liked, replied or engaged.

When the last person stops commenting, I've got another 60 seconds before Facebook says: "We'll show it to 20 more people." After that, they show it to 50 more people and then 100 more people. This process keeps going until a minute expires. Then your post is removed from the newsfeed. The only way a person can find it after that is to go to your profile. However, there is a way to restart the clock.

How many of you have scrolled through Facebook only to see a post that's two years old? Suddenly, it's right back in the feed fresh as hell. That's because somebody probably creeped your profile and liked one of your old posts.

Remember the three components of EdgeRank: weight, affinity, and time decay. These three elements of social media matter the most. And the good news is that you can always restart the clock and get your post in the newsfeed again. Here's another example. Let's say you have a good post of a house that's been for sale for three months. When you lower the price, suddenly your post will get a lot of attention. People will tell themselves: *hey, that's actually a good price.*

Maybe someone saw it earlier, and the price was too high. Well, since you lowered the price, that person gets to see the post again. They can also see that you haven't sold the property yet. Other people can see it, too. When people start replying on the post, more weight is given. This starts that call all over again, and this time, your post is shown to even more people. Your post is shown to the people who have already engaged on it, but it is also shown to their friends and friends of their friends.

That's simply phase one of your Media Marketing Method, but already, you can see that when you learn what it's all about, you can manipulate the system to get the greatest weight out of your social media marketing.

The way that you manipulate the weight is to ask the people in your groups to help you out. You want to say something like: "Can you make sure that you like this post?" We call that the whip effect because that's what happens with your post. You'll whip up supercharged results.

When you're looking to make your post stand out on Facebook, you need all three of those components. And it derives from this: the more engagement, the more successful your post. In each of these components, as I mentioned, one is not more important than the other, but the other two feed weight. Basically, weight solves most of your problems.

That's what you're posting for. To get your audience involved.

What happens if there's a price change and you have to go back and edit your post? That's okay.

Then you need to edit the original verbiage and adjust the price a tiny bit. So, you could edit it and then reply to a few people. When you do that, that will start the clock all over again.

Your replies don't really start the clock all over again, but the person you replied to will get a notification. There's a good chance that they will like your reply, or they will reply to your reply. That's what starts the clock up all over again.

Remember we can't create our own EdgeRank. We have to rely on others to do that for us. But there are still things you can do to get people to like your post. Let's say I make a comment like "What's the lowest you'll take?" but you don't reply until two weeks later.

When you do reply, you say, "We'll probably take 275 for it." When I hit the like button on your reply, it starts that time decay back over again. Every move that you make, you're looking for a way to engage people, to get them to reply.

We're in the direct response marketing world. That means we make you an offer and we're looking for a direct response from you. Everything we do is based on direct response marketing. When we make a post, our goal is to get direct responses from people.

When you use what I am sharing with you, it creates affinity. The more people who see what we have to offer, the better, and it helps our time decay as it increases our bottom line.

Chapter 2 – Timing

The EdgeRank that we talked about in the previous chapter, with the focus on Facebook, is also true for Instagram.

Instagram instituted the same algorithm about six months ago. But they are way more powerful than Facebook.

Here's an example: I have about 180K people on the Hardcore Closer fan page on Facebook. If I post on both Instagram and Facebook using the exact picture and wording on the Hardcore Closer Facebook fan page with 180K fans, I get 200 likes.

When I post that same post on Instagram where I have about 85K people, I'll get 1,000-1,500 likes and 150-200 comments. So, Instagram is where Facebook was four years ago. A lot of people run from Instagram. They think you can't make money from it. That couldn't be farther from the truth.

The same algorithm for Facebook I've explained is also true of Instagram. The people who you engage with the most on Instagram are the ones who you see in your newsfeed.

The time decay formula is also true. If somebody goes back and comments on an old Instagram post of yours, it'll put it right back in the newsfeed. The more likes, the more hearts, the more comments, the more replies, the more weight and affinity that are created and the more the time decay clock restarts. People can't do as much on Instagram as they can on Facebook, but Instagram has stories. The Instagram newsfeed is not the most popular feed; the story feed is actually viewed more.

The story feed lets you post and watch quick 15-second pictures, memes, or videos, and so if I want to skip it, I can. I don't have to invest a lot of time to read other people's posts. Stories make for a faster way to engage with people. The more people who view your stories and send you direct messages or reply to your stories the more it counts toward your EdgeRank. But it's almost as if on Instagram there are two completely different sets of EdgeRank. Because the people who see my stories are rarely the people who like my posts. I'll get between 1,500-2,500 views, but my average post gets about 500 likes. Yet on FB, I get a fraction of that.

Instagram used to be about posting pictures, but I have noticed people are starting to read what you write. So, the longer the post on Instagram the more engagement you should get.

I can now write long posts and even add spaces to them. If you don't know how to do that, it's an easy hack.

On an iPhone, if you push the "123" button on the bottom, it gives you the return option. Then you simply push the return button to divide up your content.

The longer people stare at your post, the more ways than one they have to click. They might as well leave a comment. And this all adds up to create affinity in the same way.

What we're trying to do on Instagram is the same thing we're trying to do on FB. We want to draw people to our profile. We want to nonchalantly get them to pay attention to us.

What matters the most on Instagram EdgeRank is how many people view your profile every week.

So, in the last seven days, 3,334 people have visited my profile. That means they didn't just see me in a newsfeed or watch my story. They went out of their way to go to my profile.

As people are going to my profile, I also go to theirs. Both on Instagram and Facebook. But to stay focused on Facebook, I need a little help.

Facebook can be a time suck if you don't stay focused, I use a plugin called the News Feed Eradicator. If you have Chrome, it's free. You just have to download it and then turn it on.

It edits your newsfeed, so normally, where you would have your sidebar: groups, birthdays, etc., the Eradicator gets rid of those. Then you are left with the main feed in the middle of the page.

I have one job and one job only and that is to get people to look at my profile or posts. I don't want to get caught up looking at other people. Now, I can always go to anybody's profile—those top 25-50 people who I want to engage with—and I can make sure they're seeing my posts. And if I want to see them, I can always type their name in and go to their profile, but this plugin keeps me even more on my game.

I'm at a point now where I have 30,000 people on my personal page, so for me to come up with 25 to 50 people, is kind of irrelevant. Enough people see me now, and we have leads coming in on a regular basis.

But just because that is my personal situation right now, I don't want you to think *until I get to where Ryan's at it won't be like that for me.*

I had to start from zero, too. But I have consistently done what I'm telling you about for 10 years. That's me posting crazy-ass stories and getting kicked off Facebook for telling people off. Keeping that in mind, you can get ahead a lot faster if you follow the system in this book.

I use the News Feed Eradicator to allow my focus to remain on creating EdgeRank in groups, too. It works because the Sales Talk With Sales Pro group has 80K people. I know if I can create that affinity, time decay and weight inside of that group, when I post there, most of the 80K members are going to see what I post.

When I go to Sales Pitches Galore which has 10,000 people in it, and I get a lot of engagement, that group has affinity with me, which shows exponentially more people my content versus my newsfeed. Plus, people see it in their newsfeed.

But besides simply posting in the group, I want to walk you deeper into the process.

I've saved a small collection of groups, and every morning when I get up, I drop a blog post in one group, and a different blog post in another group, and so on. After I do that for about 10 minutes, I'm done with social media for the morning. My goal in the morning is to make the steps I take meaningful. Whatever I am doing, I'm constantly creating affinity within those groups. Let's say that you have 300-400 friends on your FB page. The easiest way to get more friends is to engage in groups where the people you want to do business with most likely are.

Plenty of people come through our program and have become pros. People start to know who you are. In the groups, someone might post: "Who in here who builds funnels?" Then people are tagged. Another person might post: "Who in here does credit repair?" People tag Billy Alt all the time because he has followed this process and gotten active in groups. And other people have done the same. Because of that, they've built huge followings.

This is far more effective than saying, "Hey, go like my page. Let's be friends." And it's all because we are consistently adding value.

I know that most of my clients are up by 6:30 a.m., especially since I teach people to get up, go to the gym, bust your ass at work and then shut work off and spend time with your family. That's the process that I've been teaching for a few years now. Most of the people I work with wake up early in the morning.

I'm inside my perfect client's head now, and this is what you've got to do, too. You've got to dial in who you want to attract and who you want to engage with. Because if you sell small business consulting, and every broke-dick who hasn't even started a business sees your post, it doesn't do you any good. Take the time to get into the eyes and the mind of the small business owner.

This is what the small business owner faces every day when they wake up. They'll have an employee who quits. Somebody will call in sick. Unexpected bullshit will happen at work; a surprise bill will pop up and that all creates drama. But it's all just a part of owning a business.

The majority of my clients are in sales and are small business owners. They are entrepreneurs and coaches. I know their mindset, and I make sure they see my content.

At 6:30 every morning, I type out a motivational post. That's also the reason why I created the Get Your Mind Right podcast. We tell everybody to listen to it as soon as they wake up every morning. The people who do, have changed their lives. I recorded episode 104 this morning, and it takes me about five minutes. The podcast is absolutely free. I put it together because I know the people who are high performers are the people who follow me.

If we get our mind right first thing in the morning, then we have motivation to carry us through the day. I also know that it's 6:30 in the morning; we're still fuzzy. If I make offers to buy houses or products, asking for people to give me $5,000, it won't work.

They'd think: *I've barely woken up. Man, he's already hitting sales pitches.* They're not going to respond to those pitches, but I know they do want motivation first thing in the morning. So, I've created this following of people who go to my page as soon as they wake up. They read my posts first because they know, I am not bringing drama. They know what I share will not be uninspiring. It will not be demeaning. They know what I post is what they want to read.

I'm in the mind of my audience.

When I wake up and get into the office, I follow a schedule. I drink some water, and then I sit down and get my head together for a few minutes.

I log into my laptop and type out my morning post, and I know I need to write something that's inspiring.

At this point, you might be thinking *Ryan you have this innate ability to create content*. And a lot of people start to make excuses about why it would work for me and not them. But I do need to find ways to create inspiration as well.

Since it would be weird for me to listen to the Get Your Mind Right podcast, and I can imagine somebody going: "I caught Stewman listening to his own podcast; what a narcissistic bastard," I can't do that.

As an artist, for some reason, you're not supposed to do that. It would be like if you saw Chris Brown rollin' in his car, jammin' to his own song.

Instead of listening to my own stuff, I listen to people like Ed Mylett, Tony Robbins, Eric Thomas, Les Brown and Grant Cardone. I listen to the big names, but I also listen to people that not many have heard of. Nick Santo is one of those dudes. He's got one arm, no legs and no excuses.

I met Nick when I spoke at Funnel Hacking. He is a man who has embraced the FYE lifestyle. This was long before I had even branded FYE.

This dude has every reason to be rolling around in a wheelchair with his hand out, trying to get people to give him money. Instead, he gives motivational speeches about "if I can do it, you can do it."

He always challenges himself, too, saying "I talk to the prettiest girls even though I have these deformities. I was a wrestler in high school, and I was able to pin people that had two legs and two arms, and I was able to wrap my one arm around him and get on top of him and pin him."

One morning as I was listening to him; I was inspired. So, I got on Facebook and made a quick post that said: "Does anybody else have this relentless lifestyle that they're following? I call it the No Limit lifestyle."

You can do this, too. When you're getting up in the morning, I recommend following this routine because people who sleep late are probably not your ideal clients anyway. We're trying to work with hustlers.

Plenty of nights I've gotten in at 2:00 in the morning because the wife and I have been partying. We are very socially active, and no matter what I do I'm still up at 6:00 a.m. without an alarm clock. I'm just naturally wired that way. Most of the people in my programs who I'm connected with are that way, too. I can call any of my business partners, investors, or any of the people who are on my staff at 6:30 in the morning and they'll answer their phone. That's just the way we are.

I recommend that you start making motivational posts first thing in the morning. Wake up and listen to my podcasts. Watch one of my videos or watch videos and engage with the content of the people I just named. Listen to podcasts, write something...anything to get started on this new schedule and see what happens. But don't write negative news because if you do that, it will kill you.

There's one thing I hate about this building. I mean, I love our office building; and we pay a shitload of rent, so it's nice. But I hate it when I get off the elevator, and CNN's on the TV. As I walk through the corridor, it's nothing but Trump bashing all day long.

I don't give a fuck if you like the guy or not, but I don't want to hear about him 24/7. I can imagine the mindsets of the people who walk through here every morning, and it's all they've seen.

They're probably thinking, *these Trump supporters, what haters.* Then there's turmoil in the office because of what they've been exposed to. I watch people in the gym staring at the TV. When they leave, they have a mean demeanor. Their expression is as if the world's coming to an end. But we live in a safe time. In fact, it is the safest time to be alive. A buddy and I drove a $200,000 car into crack house territory in Dallas the other day, and everybody was nice to us. They walked up to us and said, "What's up, man? What're you guys doing down here? You guys looking for properties?" There were cameras everywhere, so crime's at an all-time low. That's what I mean by it's a very safe time to be alive. The news will have you believe otherwise. But just as I did on my Facebook feed with the Eradicator, I decided a long time ago that I would stop watching the news. There's a weather app on my phone if I need it. Or I just look outside. *Right, it's another hot day in Texas.* It rains in April, and it's mainly scorching the rest of the year. So, instead of waking up and listening to Fox News or CNN which gets people all triggered and pissed, I want to be the person to trigger them to be inspired. You don't have to get out of bed and subject yourself to CNN; you can listen to me. CNBC has the same effect as any of the news, and even SportsCenter is on my shit list because the bad news is sprinkled in everywhere.

When you listen to motivational content first thing in the morning, you will probably also come up with business ideas, or other brainstorms. That happens to me.

I get fired up to share what I thought of with my network because my client is there.

The average business owner, entrepreneur, and top salesperson is grinding from 9:00 to 5:00, which means I have to hit them up at 6:30 before they get in the car. As soon as they get in the car, they're trying to psych themselves out of running everybody off the road. I don't know where you live but we have lots of people moving to Dallas and they can't build the roads fast enough.

As soon as these top performers get in the car, they start thinking about everything they have to do for the day. Then as soon as they get into the office, they are overwhelmed with everything piled on their desk. They're busy as hell. Maybe they take a break for lunch, but many of us don't. There are many days when I look up at the clock, and it's already three o'clock. I haven't even gotten up from my freaking desk to use the restroom. I've just been tied to the damn thing...which brings me to why I post at 4:30 p.m. for the second time that day. I know at 4:30 p.m., two things are happening: People are getting ready for the end of the day, and if they're my perfect customer they've preloaded their day, which means they've gotten all the hard work out of the way as fast as they possibly could.

With that work off their plate, they're usually free by 4:30 in the afternoon. They will be transitioning into a different part of their day. I don't always post at 4:30 only; sometimes, I may make a post at lunch. I might have a good idea or maybe something funny happened, and I will tell that story.

To recap the clockwork: I post something inspirational at about 6:30 in the morning and then again at 4:30 in the afternoon (some days, I post at lunch).

In the afternoon, I don't need to motivate you anymore; I need to entertain you. So, at 4:30, I try to come up with funny content. Fortunately for me, humor comes naturally. Since I had a really messed-up childhood, I learned to deal with it through humor, and oftentimes, inappropriate humor. So, I share my funny perspectives online. If you guys aren't naturally funny, or entertaining, check out *People Magazine.* Find out what's going on. If you mainly sell to dudes, then you need a tactic they will respond to.

According to Instagram and Facebook, 73 percent of the people who look at my stuff are men, so I'm obviously not going to talk about the Kardashians. None of my people would care. I do know this. If you sell houses, you want to appeal to women.

Here's why. In my house, the person who makes the decision about where we live is not me; it's my wife. If it were up to me, we'd still live in the penthouse.

When we were moving from the penthouse, it was because she said, "We have a cat. We need a house." I said, "No, no; I'm not moving to the suburbs." She said, "I think we need to move to Plano."

Me: I'm from Dallas. I'm not moving to Plano. They have cops up there who actually care about their people. They write speeding tickets.

Amy: We're going to have to move to Plano.

So, we moved to Plano. Once we had lived there for two years, she said, "I think we need a bigger house."

I was like, "This house is big enough. I like the bills here."

My house, at the time, cost me $2,000 a month in mortgage and my penthouse was $8,000 a month. I liked that change. I liked those savings.

We had a really nice house; worth about $600K, and 3,400 square feet. We put a lot of work into it and about the time I was putting the finishing touches on it, Amy said, "I think we need a bigger house. When we moved into this house, we didn't have Colton. Now we have three kids and four bedrooms..."

Me: Right! We have a kid in each room. It's perfect!

Amy: I think we need an extra bedroom for our family.

Me: Problem solved. They are not sleeping at my house.

When we go to their place, and we stay in Kansas or Florida, we rent a hotel. We don't like to impose.

The end result of this conversation is that you should always know who you are selling to. I just told you what kind of clients Amy and I are. And we have since moved.

I know at the end of the day salespeople have had a rough day. They've been told off. They've had orders canceled. Business owners have been pissed off at them, and so they've had to do damage control. So, I know at 4:30 I need to lighten the mood.

I'm aiming to give them entertaining posts. Maybe I'll talk about sports. Maybe I'll talk about humor as I mentioned. If you want more inspiration, you can go to a site called Reddit.com. Reddit is a site that will give you topics that you can use for inspiration to write your posts.

There's one thread on Reddit called shower thoughts, and it has some of the funniest stuff you will ever read in your life. You know how when you're alone in the shower, a ridiculous thought crops up in your mind? That's what this thread is all about.

There are thousands upon thousands of posts. I usually scroll through that thread when I'm out of ideas. BuzzFeed is another source you can pull from. They're getting political lately, so you need to watch that, but usually, there's a lot of funny content you can grab from there, too.

Again, I'm just trying to lighten the mood. I'm trying to let the people reading my posts know I understand. *I know you had a rough day. You worked your ass off all damn day long. Let me make it a little easier on you.* The last post I make for the day is at 8 o'clock at night.

My 8 p.m. post is when I make my offers. I know it's the end of the day and people are probably still sitting on their couch with their wallets in their back pocket. Think about it. At eight o'clock you haven't quite gotten out of your clothes for the day. A lot of people go home and eat dinner still dressed from work. They have their wallets in their back pockets. That's important. If I am going to make sales, I need them to have access to that piece of plastic.

My post might read something like "Tonight, you can get in on this offer (then I explain the offer)." It's short and sweet, and I don't post about offers every single day. I alternate what I am posting because if I'm constantly making offers at 8 p.m., then people are not going to check my page at 8 p.m. They would assume I was trying to sell them something. If I did that during the day, and then at 8 p.m., I would doom myself.

So, I switch it up on them, but every day, I make sure that I follow these two post rules, and about every other day I make offers at 8 p.m. But I still do post every day at 8 p.m. even if I am not sharing offers.

The best time for me to make offers is on the weekends at 4:30. Why? The same reasoning applies. You're still sitting around somewhere with your wallet in your back pocket, so if I can make an offer, you will be more likely to take me up on it. Plus, if you're in my audience, you're probably about two or three beers in, and maybe you've had a joint or two. You're more open to making purchases. Your guard is down a little bit.

The next thing you know, you're sitting in front of me at an event.

At 8 p.m. on a Sunday especially, people might know that they had a good week and so you can catch them then. Friday at that time also works to make an offer or two. If they had a shitty week, they might need my help. If they had a good week; they made money, and so they might even want more help. On Fridays,

Saturdays and Sundays, I'm trying to make sure that I put offers in front of people. But since I'm going through groups, I'll alternate my offers there.

This means I'm literally making an offer every day, but it might be on my profile page. I alternate the postings there, too.

Now again, I can't just go into anybody's group and tell them to buy my stuff. You have to know the path to do that, and you need to work with the admins so that you have permission to post in their groups as well. I can do it in my own groups because I assume everybody knows who the hell I am and so I shouldn't have to explain why I'm making offers. So far, I haven't been met with much confrontation.

Still, I go inside of other people's groups. When you show up in these groups, the best way to do that is to present value, just as you would do in your own groups.

You don't have to only post offers in a group either. Let's say I own a landscape business and this week we grew our business from 50 yards to 150 yards. I've had to hire two more people, and I've learned how to scale. You might post in a group: "I've always wondered if there are other landscapers that struggle with XYZ as well." Once you post that, people will hit you up and engage with you. A lot of people will send you a direct message, and they'll say, "Can you teach me how to do that?" My response is "Yeah, I can absolutely!" That's exactly what we're trying to do. My number one job is to take people from watching my profile to hitting me up in direct message because that's where I make 99% of my sales.

I check Facebook Messenger more than I check my email, which is ironic because so many people don't want to use messenger.

Understand, I'm not going to give people free information.

Many times, people will say to me, "Can you mentor me? You know I need a free mentor." And I will reply "Dude, I got your free mentor right here. Just go to HardcoreCloser.com/Blog, and you'll find whatever you need." I'll pawn them off, and they might read a few posts on my site and make $1.00 from it.

They might also say, "I have a thousand dollars to spend, which one of your programs would be the best for me?" This happens all the time because I'm providing value constantly. This is precisely why I'm trying to drive everybody into my direct messenger. When I open my messages, I know those people are the most serious about buying my products.

People in your DM have gone out of their way to send you a message. Since they have taken those extra steps and that effort, you know they want to talk to you; they want to ask you specific questions.

That's a well-qualified prospect.

And did you know, there's a spam filter in your direct messages? You can find even more people who are trying to make contact with you there.

So, you have to make sure that you check those spam messages every day—especially if you're active in groups. People who aren't your friends will automatically go into that spam filter. A prospect might be waiting there for you.

Every day I bet I find 10 or 15 messages in that folder. The same goes for Instagram. They have a folder where people who've contacted you but have not connected with you go. I make a lot of money in my DMs on Instagram as well.

Facebook and Instagram have the biggest pool of prospects on the internet, so the people who are reaching out to you are reaching out for a reason.

Last night, a few people hit me up about a house I'm selling in South Dallas. I got it for 40 grand. People submit applications to us because we target people who are on the foreclosure list. We let them know if you live in Texas, and your home is up for foreclosure, that means the first Tuesday of next month the government will kick you out and put all your belongings in the front yard. You'll be out of a house.

If you want an appointment to keep that foreclosure off your credit, then we can give you up to $25,000 to sell us your house. We will pay for your move and will even let you live in the house for another 30 days until you figure out where you're going. All you have to do is fill out an application.

That's the gist of the ad we run the last two weeks of every month and people are always hitting us up. That's how I found this house I'm selling.

It's worth about $120K, but it needs about 20 grand worth of work. At that price, you know it's obviously a small house, so 20 grand goes a long way in an 800-

900 square foot home. It's definitely in the hood, but it's a good fix and flip or rental.

Probably 10 people hit me up about that house when I posted about it.

From that post, three people are going out to look at it to decide whether they want to buy it.

I don't constantly advertise coaching either. But I do it a lot. Break Free Academy is still my main source of income. But last month all my companies did about $2.3 million in transactions. Some of that's real estate, so I know after running the numbers we usually make $150K in profit per transaction.

The point is that I'm running regular businesses in various industries using the techniques I am teaching you.

I'm intentional, and I will not be distracted because one of the most powerful tools that we have on this planet is our focus.

Focus is a huge key that you need to tap into that will enable this method to work.

Since birth, everything on this planet has been trying to distract you and tell you that you can't pay attention. When class was boring, what did they tell you? They said you had attention deficit disorder (ADD) or attention deficit hyperactivity disorder (ADHD). I always thought, *maybe I don't have ADD maybe your math lesson sucks? Maybe it's boring.*

My kids go to private school for one reason and one reason only.

It's not because I like spending money, because I don't. You can ask people who know me. I'm very tight with my money.

I put my kids in private school because I feel like those people work for me, so they can't put labels on my kids because I'm paying them. In public school they don't give a shit about your kids, but in private school, I can have a conversation with a teacher. I can say, "My kid's special." And the teachers and administrators have to take it at face value, or they're not going to get my $30,000. It gives me a different relationship with them. When I was growing up, people would say, "He has attention deficit disorder." That was not true because I could sit down and play video games for hours at a time and they would have 100% of my attention. I can also go fishing for hours at a time.

Which leads me to my point. When I write a blog post, I give it 100% of my attention. Of course, that makes sense because those are activities I like doing. The world tries to tell you that you have ADD because you are attempting to do something that you don't like.

We say things like "I'm a salesman. I don't pay attention to details." Don't you hear salespeople say that all the time? Well, we know what the world tries to impose on us is powerful because we start to believe it—even if it's not true.

The most powerful weapon that we have on this planet is focus.

The law of attraction even revolves around the concept of focus.

You get what you focus on. The Bible even references this law as being true, stating, "Faith without works is dead."

You have to do the work. To accomplish the work, you must maintain focus. Remember, if you are interested in what you are doing, you will maintain the focus needed to reach your goal.

Take Facebook. Facebook's no different than anything else the world is trying to use to distract us.

Did you know we see 4,000 advertisements every day?

An advertisement is nothing more than a distraction.

In a normal day, you might be focused on completing a job, but then you would see an ad. That's one time. If every day you are distracted 4,000 times, you've got 3,999 distractions to go!

This is why you need to get focused on what works for you.

If I didn't have the News Feed Eradicator, the 10 minutes that it would take me to post in all those groups and write the post on my personal page would turn into an hour. I'd miss the gym and everything else I was supposed to do.

I use everything within me and every ace I'm holding onto to focus every chance I get. Set yourself up for success when you go on social media. You might find the rule of using your phone for social media fun, but your desktop and laptop for social media work helpful. When I make these rules, then I can hit the groups I want to hit, and I make sure my work is done.

I also set alarms that go off to remind me every day to make sure that I post at these specific times. These days, I'm pretty damn routine, and I'm used to that schedule. Now, I don't need the alarms as much because what I do has become a habit.

When I first started this routine, I set an alarm every day to write down my daily wins. That's what I told myself as one of the reasons I was sticking to a schedule. I could keep track of how I was winning through my posts.

I can go back and look at the times I have posted and read my wins. At 7:30 every day, I can read what I have written, and all the interaction that came from it. This makes me feel better if I am depressed, down, or distracted. I will read my posts and remember if I had a bad month, bad day, or a fight with the wife or the kids have decided to not listen to me. That journal gives me the ability to read all the wins that I've had every single day. I can tell myself I'm a winner and everything else going on won't affect me as much.

With those alarms, I'm 100% focused. I live my life by a calendar with the alarms going off at different points of the day.

You have to be this deliberate with what you are doing because if you're not careful, social media (and everything else) will distract the hell outta you and your pay will be affected. You'll be keeping up with Infowars instead of doing what you're supposed to be doing.

No one wants that. You want to make sure that you are on social media for business purposes only, that you're not distracted and that you're in and out.

If I make a post at 6:30 in the morning I don't have to watch it all day. Whoever replied at 7:30 is still going to be there at lunchtime when I'm in line waiting for food, and I can reply then.

You can answer when you have a spare moment. You can even be in the bathroom. You don't have to babysit your posts.

Maybe you make a post at 6:30, and another one at 4:30 in the afternoon. Once you go home and after you've settled your kids in at the end of the night you can go back, and reply. When you start talking and engaging with everybody on that earlier post, it starts that time decay clock all over again.

I run eight companies. If I were on social media all the time, I would be broke as hell. I would have eight bankrupt companies. That's why I have a system that makes it look like I'm omnipresent. Really, I'm not.

I am on messenger all the time, however. I treat it just like my emails.

I can access it at any time no matter what I'm doing. When I'm recording, on a call, doing a podcast, writing a blog post, looking at properties, whatever the case is, I can answer that DM.

You don't have to spend all your time on social media. You can also come up with a schedule that will make it okay for you to be off there more and to get more work done.

Back to the when and why of the posting schedule.

Once the average person is done for the day, and they are at home and comfortable, they will start looking for luxury items. This is when they are loan shopping, trying to find a mortgage guy. Your client might be a house flipper out in the field all day, making bids. But when he gets home at night, he'll scroll Facebook to find other deals.

A person who's getting engaged or who wants to buy diamonds like my wife does might shop at the end of the night. I'm the same way. I get home, get in bed, and I don't watch TV, so Amy will have a show playing in the background, and I'll get on my phone, too.

Before I go to sleep, I'll start looking for watches and browse other stuff that I want to spend my money on, even though I don't pull the trigger. It's just window shopping, or phone shopping, I guess we could call it.

Most people who are buying those kinds of goods don't do it until the end of the day. Even though that is the case, you still must keep them engaged throughout the day, so they constantly go back to your page. It's just like any other direct marketing effort.

We're trying to drive traffic to our profile page. If people see us in the newsfeed we want to have made a big enough impact on them, so they'll wonder what we're up to and visit our profile.

Then they'll go back to our page and comment. They'll start engaging on older posts, and as you know, that starts the time decay over again.

When you conduct yourself like this on social media, it's a smart move because people will think they can easily reach out to you. That's what you want, but you also need to practice the schedule where you are not constantly on these platforms. That is the schedule that will allow you to work and make the most of your time and money.

Chapter 3 – Hierarchy of the Post

Since the dawn of time, the process I'm about to explain to you has worked across all communication platforms. It has worked ever since people were writing on rice paper in Egypt.

If you search on social media, you'll see 5-10 posts from your friends and fan pages, and then you'll see an advertisement from someone like me. The same thing applies to Instagram, Twitter and YouTube. You'll watch three or four videos, and then you'll have to go through an ad process before you can watch the next video. That is unless you pay $10/month. If you do that, then you don't have to watch any ads.

The media has a rule. If they give you what you want 80% of the time, then they can take whatever they need to pay the bills 20% of the time. We use the 80/20 rule inside of M3, and we call it the whip effect.

If you adopt this to how you do social media, you can get away with as many advertisements as you want within that 20%.

Let's say that we're making three posts a day on Facebook and Instagram. We'll do one news feed post a day like a video or a picture and four or five stories. I always do more stories than posts because the stories expire every 24 hours.

So, make three posts a day on your personal page; you want to cover morning noon and night because some people only get on their social media every other day. As a matter of fact, one of the reasons Facebook's lost $190B in market cap in the last 10 days is that people aren't using it as much.

The 80/20 rule specifies that out of every five posts one is an ad. This means you should put offers on your page every other day, but it doesn't mean you have to keep it to a science. That fifth post doesn't always have to be an ad; just make sure the ratio is right.

I may make up to six posts in a single day, but when I do, I make sure that I don't just make posts for post's sake. I'm making sure they're quality and that my people actually enjoy reading them. This is why I advise posting in groups.

Ask the admin of the group what you can do to become a moderator in the group. A moderator can't kick people out of the group or take over the group. You'll have limited access to the group as a moderator, but you will be able to delete posts and comments, etc. You can tell them that you have a lot of good content to share. Let the admin know that you can help them out in a different way, too. Try asking the admin this question: "What's one thing that really annoys you about this group that I can help you with?" Most of the time the admin will tell you that they could use a hand managing the spam.

They will be grateful if you can help them with that problem, and you can figure out an arrangement where in exchange you can be a moderator. As a moderator, you'll get a little badge that allows you to post with authority, which helps your posts to be viewed more as well. If you post in that group three times a day and two of those times are solid posts, then you can create a huge following. That's how I reached 30,000 followers on my personal Facebook page. I've been reaching out to admins forever. Another bonus is once you build your own group, you can tell the admins "I've got a group with 5,000 people in it, and I'll let you cross-pollinate. You can add content and make offers to my group as long as I can come into yours."

If you strike this deal, then make sure you follow the schedule that every third post needs to be an ad whether it's in a group, or on your page. If you had a good day and were on a roll, and made five or six posts throughout the day, if you drop an ad in, that's fine.

An example of an offer could be, "If you're looking for a home in Austin, here's a link that lets you search houses absolutely free. You don't even have to opt-in to see new listings in your area." Or, "Here's a new listing for an open house this weekend." Your offers don't have to be as direct as "buy my stuff." They can be nonchalant. I give testimonials as offers. I tell a story about the results a client got through my program. At the end of the post, I'll say something like: "If you'd like to talk about how to start this process, just hit me up in the DM." I tell people to personally hit me up in the DM because I have noticed that when people comment, there are always roaches trying to undercut you.

The Hierarchy of the Post

If we're advertising on Alexa or in holographic form, or virtual reality one day, what I am sharing with you will still work. So, after you read this chapter and this book, you can take it with you for the rest of your life.

If you start writing for a magazine it applies. If you start doing a podcast, it also applies. On my podcast, we load it, so the first 10 minutes of the podcast is a commercial. During that time, we're asking for reviews. I'm doing a commercial for PhoneSites. The remaining 80% of the podcast is all content. I follow that process religiously across every platform that I use, and that's what's built me the following I have. I constantly get people to take me up on my offers, and your goal is to do the same.

Structuring our media this way doesn't cost us a dime. It just takes a bit of our time. You should also know that you don't want to do this with Hootsuite or Buffer either.

Facebook cares about the amount of time you spend on their site, so if you go through Hootsuite or any other third-party posting service, FB knows you're not on their site. When they recognize this, they are not going to help you out by letting people see you because you're not allowing them to advertise.

Remember also, 80% of the people that are on Facebook look at the site on a mobile device, not a desktop. You may also want to use what's called instant articles, although I haven't done this with any of my companies.

How Facebook determines if your content is good and warrants views is what we call the hierarchy of the post. This simply means that Facebook likes certain content more than others.

If you make the posts that Facebook likes, they're more likely to show up in the newsfeed which is the whole point of everything I've gone over so far. We want people to know who you are because people buy from people they know, like and trust. That means we have to get into the newsfeed of the people we want most to connect with. Knowing the hierarchy of posts is useful because then you can post the types of content that are more likely to be seen by more people in the newsfeed.

The first thing that Facebook loves more than anything else Is live video.

Every time you turn that video on and you flip it around, GPS trackers inside that app are gathering information about what the room inside the building you are in looks like. At some point in the future, if the FBI needed to raid that building, they've already mapped the entire building out. Their software knows where every door is, etc.

Live videos are unfiltered social media—where people are connecting and getting to know each other. Think of it like your own reality show.

The average live video time needs to be seven minutes-plus. If you make a quick 3-4-minute live video that's not enough time for people to get on board.

Aim for making a live video post once a day across all platforms and then two a week on YouTube. When you first go live, say, "Hey, it's (your name). Can you give me some hearts, give some thumbs ups? Let's get it engaged. Let's get people on here." Then you can start reading people's comments. When you do this, people want to comment, so their name will be read out loud in front of everybody. Doing this also creates weight. You want to stay on for seven minutes because the second your live video pops up everybody on Facebook doesn't rush to view it. You have to give it a few minutes. When you go live, Facebook's trying to identify the best available audience who want to watch the live video. The quicker you get those people engaged, the faster your time decay will start all over again.

You want to engage your viewers. "Leave me a comment if this has ever happened to you. See? It's happened to John. It's happened to Brad. It's happened to Sam." It might seem like a simple tactic, but by doing that, you are creating more and more weight. More people are commenting and engaging, and that means FB is showing your video to more and more people. Facebook is thinking *damn this video is getting a lot of engagement*.

The biggest mistake I see people making is that they turn on the live video and they immediately start telling the story right away. They don't engage the audience, and then they shut their video off.

I usually let the video run for about 30 seconds before I even say anything. If you think about it, it takes people a couple of minutes to write a few paragraphs. So, if you let your video run for 7-15 minutes, you might have 100 people hit the heart or the thumbs up. Maybe only 10 people are watching but they might have each hit those emojis 10 times, and that still counts. Once you're done, Facebook tallies up the weight and the engagement and shows it to more people. Even though it's not live anymore, people will leave comments, and this creates a massive amount of weight. That's why live videos get the exposure they do, but I really can't stress strongly enough that you need to make sure that they're seven minutes or longer.

The next thing that gets engagement on FB is the long-form post, and this is three-plus paragraphs. Most people usually write one or two sentences, but if you can articulate your point, a couple of things will happen. The people who are scrolling will stop and read your post, which keeps them on Facebook a little bit longer. That gives Facebook the right to serve up an ad. Plus if we know that clicking "see more" is a form of weight and engagement; then your long-form paragraph is almost the same as that live video. When I write a big-ass hook headline that draws people in, I hide my sales pitch, so people have to click "see more" to read it. This is why you never want to open up a long-form post with a sales pitch. Because people will never click "see more."

Here's an example of a well-structured long-form post: "You can make $100,000 in the next 31 days following a really simple method. It's as simple as doing one thing, etc." When your reader clicks "see more" then they'll see a few bullet points and an offer at the bottom. At that point, they're so engaged on it, and they've already clicked on your post that Facebook will show it to more people. That's why every single morning you'll see me write 3-5 paragraphs. I'm getting people engaged, and when I make an offer, you'll never see me leave links on FB. That's what that long-form post is for.

After I post the link all the way at the bottom of the post, then I delete the preview screenshot of the link by hitting the X in the upper right-hand corner. Now, I have a long post with a hidden link, and I am not penalized for having that link and potentially taking people off Facebook.

All I am doing is following the 80-20 rule. Eighty percent of those three-plus paragraphs is good content. Twenty percent will be a sales pitch.

Facebook loves long-form posts because people get stuck in that white box.

As we discuss engagement further, you should understand that Facebook has decided to throttle business pages. They're putting us in a pay-to-play situation. If you're not running ads from your business page, it's really not doing you any good unless your page is viral.

More than ever, Facebook is showing people your organic posts—meaning the content is coming from your personal Facebook page.

If you have a business page, you should be putting offers out all the damn time. This is a business page, and your followers should expect that.

On that same topic and before I get back to discussing your personal page, you should also know that you can view the ads your competitor is running.

If you know that Zillow runs ads, for instance, and you want to mimic them, you can do that. On your mobile app, go to any business page, and in the bottom right corner, there's a little eye. Click that eye and it will bring up the all the ads the page is running.

Then you can customize that ad for yourself.

It doesn't tell you the audience, but you will still have that info.

Again, we are zeroing in on using your organic content, and with that in mind, maybe you want to be a better writer. Maybe you want to improve the content on your personal Instagram or Facebook pages.

You can try these three things:

Number one: write. If you went to Hardcore Closer 4-5 years ago, my blog was boring. My writing skills weren't sharp. But now, I write sometimes, 10,000 words a day. At the very least, I'll write 5,000. All of that practice means I've gotten really good at articulating.

When you write, you don't want to write above a fifth-grade level.

Remember the concept of Keeping It Simple Sales. Anyone can understand the fifth-grade level.

Number two: Don't write for an audience. Write for one person. If you have 1,000 friends on Facebook, 400-500 of them will be on the same wavelength as you, communication-wise, but you'll lose the other half. When I write every post on Facebook, I'm talking to a guy named Mike. I've got him in my mind. It's just Mike and me having a conversation. If I tried to speak to my entire following, people would wonder, *who's he talking to?* Writing like this has helped me reach more people. Almost every day, I get messages from people who say that I wrote a post just for them.

When you write blast emails if you're trying to write them as if you're talking to every gender, race, creed, color, religion, you ought to speak to a specific person.

A book called *Kick-Ass Copywriting Secrets of a Marketing Rebel* written by John Carlton is an excellent resource for you.

Carlton recommends that you imagine as you're writing that you have a gun to your head. If your offer doesn't convert that trigger will get pulled. When you think this way, it makes you work harder. It makes your writing mean more.

Both John Carlton and Dan Kennedy are the kings of direct response marketing, and they teach people how to write the long-form post. Back when they got started, they wrote blog posts and sales letters, but we now have the ability to do that on Facebook.

Third: use a software called Grammarly, which is a free app you can download to Chrome, Safari, your phone and even Word. Grammarly makes your writing friendlier. It will give you alerts when your writing is too complex and too hard to understand. It'll tell you where to go back and make suggestions almost like your old English teacher.

When someone is writing overly smart content, it's boring because it gives you too much to think about. We're used to mind-numbing content we are bombarded with every day: the TV, radio, YouTube and everywhere else.

But we're selling to the masses and we have to remember that. There's a book called *Ogilvy on Advertising* by David Ogilvy. He is the king of copywriting, and the show *Mad Men* is based on him. His famous saying is: "The consumer isn't some rocket scientist. That consumer's your wife, and your mom, and so you want to communicate with your consumers the same way you communicate with your wife and your mom."

Returning to the topic of the hierarchy of the post, next on the list is pre-recorded videos.

Pre-recorded videos don't get near the amount of engagement as live videos and long-form posts.

Have you noticed, you don't get alerts for just anything, but you do get alerts for live videos on a regular basis. Now that you know this, you'll start seeing more and more of those in your newsfeed than before. Yes, Facebook loves live videos more than the canned ones. People aren't doing as many as they used to anyway, and so you don't see a whole lot of them. Lives have taken over.

When I first started Facebook marketing I had to record the selfie video and then upload it to Facebook because they didn't have live yet. Now, that lives are available, most people live stream them, but canned videos are still very beneficial.

Photos and memes come right after canned videos in the list. I'm sure you'll agree that memes are pretty popular. We live in a meme culture. Memes are hilarious; they're motivational and cool. But they burn out in Facebook's eyes after a while. Facebook has a database where they store every picture that's ever been on Facebook or Instagram. When a meme has been maxed out, Facebook puts the kibosh on it, and starts limiting the views.

But if you want to reinvigorate a meme, try this hack. Don't download the photo. Instead, screenshot it, and change the filter and the dimensions. Then when you upload it to your page, Facebook will treat it as if it's a whole new image.

People will share your meme and it's okay to share other people's memes especially if they have their name or logo.

The other way that you can get engagement on your pictures is to use shots of your family or cars. I take photos of cars or my wife. She's very pretty, and so that works really well. My baby's pictures work because people think he's really cute. Mix up what you're showing. You don't always want to share kids and wives. Every third or fifth post could be a house that you've sold, or it could be people holding sold signs or keys to a house. Give your audience some variety.

Yes, use original pictures but use pictures that will catch people's attention. Once upon a time, people would take pictures of their food, but nobody cares about that anymore. The same thing has happened with people taking pictures of themselves in the gym. Nobody cares about that, so don't do that. Make it emotional, so people get attached to you and your message. Take them on a trip down memory lane. When someone buys a house, and you take a picture of them that's a momentous occasion for people, and it takes them back in their mind: *I remember when I got the keys to my house*, etc.

Next up on the list is the short-form text, which is about 3-7 sentences. I'm not saying Facebook doesn't like short-form; I'm just noting the hierarchy of what it does like. But if you make a one or two sentence post, then make sure you ask a question. Make sure it's not a statement. You might even want to attach a photo to it or even a video.

And now Facebook hates YouTube because that's their competition, so if you share a YouTube link to Facebook you might as well keep that to yourself, for all the engagement you will get out of it. People won't click links and then go back and like and comment. People usually click links, read what was on there and then they move on.

A million people might have clicked on your link but if they did Facebook doesn't tell you how many people clicked or how many people saw your link. You will not be rewarded for trying to move people off Facebook.

To get the engagement you want, try doing one live video a week; get a lot of engagement and ask people to chime in.

I stream live from my business page, and get 2,000-3,000 people to watch my live videos on Hardcore Closer. When I'm done with that, Facebook will let me run an ad to it.

I'll let it run for about 24 hours like a live video on replay. So, people are still engaging with it and sharing it on Facebook organically. Then I'll go back and boost it for half the price and twice the engagement. Because I'm still putting money behind that live video, their algorithm identifies it as a live video. That being the case, they will show it to as many people as possible. Following this method is a cheap way to get likes, engagement and clicks from your fan pages. So, do the live video from your fan page; then let it sit for 24-48 hours. Once the engagement dies down, go back and boost it.

Here's that hierarchy again:
1. Live videos
2. Long-form posts
3. Videos

4. Photos

5. Short-form text

6. Links

We've got to leverage our content and our following to get as much out of our 20% as possible. That's where the whip effect comes in.

Combining the whip effect, with something called "the syndicate" will get your business posts seen.

If 80 percent of my content is getting a lot of engagement, but when I make an offer I'm not getting the engagement I need, I can create a syndicate to help my numbers. The best syndicate that you can create comes from networking with the people who are in the groups where you are the most active and where you give and receive the most value. I have 40 people in Push To Excellence and between 650-700 people in Entourage. Let's say I make a business offer for someone to join entourage whether in long-form or through a live video and 80% of what I am talking about is content and the last 20% is my pitch. My content will just naturally not get as much engagement because it's commercial in nature.

However, we can manipulate the algorithm on social media by creating a syndicate. The idea of the syndicate is simple. All it means is that like-minded people are conspiring to take common action. If I have a post up with an offer and 700 people have already taken me up on that offer, I can go to those 700 people and say, "Will some of y'all comment, like and engage on this post?" My weight builds up the more people that are shown the post. Then, the time decay gets another jump start.

Facebook will start showing it to more people, and then more people will read the comments. They'll think *this must be a good deal!*

You can create a syndicate through a Facebook group as well. I prefer this way instead of being chat-dependent...which can get annoying.

Remember the hierarchy of the post. Implement your syndicate to whip up your posts' engagement and improve your odds at closing more business.

Chapter 4 – Your Syndicate

Just as you establish rules when you create a group, you need to do the same when you establish a syndicate. Even if you have a chat group that helps each other out, you all need ground rules. When you set these rules, then you know that there is no sharing of dorky memes or other content that would waste the group's or syndicate's time.

Don't make your syndicate like your grandma sharing chain mails.

In my very first syndicate, I gathered up five of my most influential friends on Facebook. The plan was to be like the skull and bones of Facebook. We wanted to be the behind-the-scenes manipulators of the posts. This syndicate had rules, and you would have to hit the time stamp, copy the URL and then share it inside the group. People would write what they wanted other people to say, and so the rest of the group just had to copy the comment and paste it. They would go right down the line, and when one comment was taken, a person would move to the next one and copy and paste that one. I can literally go into the group and grab all the comments I want people to say. And as each person copied them, they hit like on the post of the next person. By managing this syndicate process in this way, I have created pre-programmed sales conversations on my posts.

When outsiders look at the post, they'll see 20 comments about the house I'm selling them. They won't realize it, but they've been sold to the whole time. I have groups with thousands of people. I ask the people in the groups to whip the posts because we know without that whip, 20% of our posts aren't going to get as much engagement since they're about business. But if more people are engaging, then you'll get your social proof.

Leverage all those vendors who come into your office and are always asking you for business. The syndicate will work with anyone in your network. You can form little groups to help each other out.

I own a software company, so people always hit me up with information about CRMs; they want to tell me about their follow up autoresponders, their email sequences and every other technical gadget or app. So, I invite them to join my group, and when I make posts, I'll give them the skinny and tell them all about the rules. I have larger groups, yes, but you can use smaller syndicates and still experience impressive results.

In the beginning, I put 10 people in a group and then I would say, "If you have something important that you want whipped, just tell me what to do, or I'll go in there and engage on it."

Leave the link in the group and turn the notifications on so that every time one of your syndicates posts in that group, you'll get a notification. And all of you should know the rule. This is the one I used: "If you post anything other than the post that you need whipped in this group then we will kick you out because we don't want it to be a fluff group that gets a bunch of notifications and distracts people. We want it to be a very specific and focused way of doing business." Because we were upfront with the rules, we never had anybody violate them. Everybody loves the rules, actually. It's the greatest arrangement because you can go in there and make a post and I can tell you guys what to say on the post, and you'll do it. After that people spend their time replying to the comments. Of course, that contributes to the EdgeRank.

I'll leave all the comments on the post. You may see a comment at 9 a.m., one at 1 p.m., one at 2:30, etc. And the comments hitting the post like that mean it bumps that time decay all day long. You have to remember that not all of us in the syndicate are online at the same time, so it's not like I make the post, and then 15 comments appear 30 seconds later. If that were the case, it wouldn't look successful anyway, but as if I'd bought fake engagement. The way that I run my syndicate and the way that I teach you to run your syndicate is to use real people who are engaging throughout the course the day. After a few days. I'll go right back to the syndicate and comment on that post: "Hey, guys here's a few more things I want you to post." That starts manipulating the algorithm again.

If you have 500 friends and let's say you work with a title company and they have 500 friends, and then your credit repair company has 500 friends, and your mortgage company has 500, all of a sudden what would've been a reach of 500 people turns into a syndicate reach of up to 2,000 people. You quadrupled your exposure simply by using a syndicate. Naturally, Facebook assumes *oh, this must be a really solid post.* And as you know, when Facebook likes a post, they might show it to 30% of the friends in the list. You can understand that this arrangement allows that post to continually and exponentially grow especially as people throughout the day or the next 24 hours engage with it.

When people comment on the post, then I will go in and reply to them as if they're a real customer asking the question. Doing that creates scarcity because if somebody likes the house (if that's what your post's about) and they see that you're commenting on it, they're better positioned to make an offer, so they don't lose out. Your post is now creating scarcity and social proof.

Dr. Robert Cialdini wrote one of the best books on sales, called *Influence.* In the book, he teaches you the six most influential ways to communicate with people and the top two are scarcity and social proof.

Here's an example of social proof: Once there was a person who was murdered in New York and everybody who witnessed it could see each other in the windows as they watched this murder happen. As a result, everyone assumed everybody else had called the police, but nobody ever did. The social proof was that they assumed everybody else had reported it because they could see the other witnesses watching as they watched. The murder was a proven fact in that group. But sadly, nobody ever said anything, so the murder went unsolved.

An example of scarcity is if you say: "This offer ends today." You might be referring to a Labor Day sale, or a Thanksgiving sale offering 50% off "today and today only." If they don't take action right now, the prospect senses that fear of missing out.

We know those are two of the biggest plays for influence and that's exactly what we're trying to do with people online. When we employ these tactics, we are influencing people to engage and buy, and we do it all by manipulating a syndicate. This also manipulates the Media Marketing Method and gets your post whipped back into the newsfeed. As a matter of fact, that's why we call it the whip effect, because if your post has floated away, then it's almost as if the whip pulls it back to the original momentum in the newsfeed.

Let's talk about the people that you should aspire to help you out.

When I wanted to be a millionaire I hired millionaire mentors and then when I wanted to get to eight figures I hired mentors who had done eight figures a year. Now, I'm trying to get to nine. Going from seven to eight isn't that hard because it's only one to ten. It's a $9 million a year difference. But to go from $10 million to $100 million is a big leap because that's a $99 million difference.

That's why I did what seemed natural, hired the people who knew how to get to those nine figures, so that I could model myself after them.

Ulysses who's in our Push To Excellence program, and who's probably the number one influencer or PR guy on the planet, helped me find the right people to be my new mentors. He said, one day, "I know you're a big Ed Mylett fan. I have him under contract, and we're doing some PR stuff for him. How would you like to write about him in Forbes?" I asked if I could interview him because he doesn't coach. And it was a good idea because Ed has an interesting story.

So, I wrote this badass article for *Influencive* telling the story about how Tony Robbins called him up and told him to up his game. It became the number one article in the history of that website with about two million shares. We also arranged for Tony Robbins, Grant Cardone and Thai Lopez to share it.

After the article hit, Ed hit me back a month or two later and said he was ready to take my money. By this time, he had gotten a group together. He told me the dates to meet for the mastermind in Coeur d'Alene where he owns property, and I committed 60 grand.

I was pretty excited to learn from these guys, too because I've never been in a room with people where the minimum barrier of entry is $10M. This was a whole new realm of millionaires to meet. So, I spent a couple of days with them. Most of them are financial planners and gym owners, which is out of my wheelhouse. These people are successful, and I learned about other businesses and strategies they are using that I can implement in my own business.

Ed's house is like Saturn with a lot of smaller houses that he owns orbiting around it. The property has waterfalls throughout and is breathtaking.

At the retreat, I was shown a whole new way of making money.

In addition, I now have new referrals. That gives me the ability to create more powerful influence in a higher-level syndicate. These are exactly the people I aspired to work with and now, they are helping me out.

You can do the same in your network.

Chapter 5 - Funnels

If 20% of your posts are going to be about business, you might as well use that 20% to capture leads.

This brings us to the topic that everyone wants to know about: funnels.

One of the benefits of using a funnel is lead generation. You can also build your CRM and automate follow up. When you do this, suddenly, you have a database. I met Jeff Bezos, the guy who owns Amazon. As I listened to him talk he said he wanted to outsource manufacturing to reduce our carbon footprint here on earth. That's where Jeff Bezos' brain is. So, your Amazon packages will come from Mars at some point. Special delivery from the red planet.

As he talked, I thought *dude, I gotta get my thinking up*. Here I am worried about how to get home in traffic, but we're going to bypass that and go straight to Mars.

Besides that, he also talked about how they made money with Amazon. The secret to their success is that Amazon built a database of people who bought books. They figured people who bought books were smarter and had more money than the average person, so they built a database of educated people. Then they started selling those people bookmarks. From there, it just exploded. When he was thinking about what else they should be selling, his answer was: "Anything we want."

When Amazon was evaluated to find out what it was worth, the value wasn't based on sales; it was based on the ability to monetize the database.

Berkshire Hathaway has quickly become the second largest real estate brokerage in America. They have also done this through the monetization of data. If you go to an Apple store, you've got to take a number and wait in line. If you go to the Microsoft Store, they might as well say, "Thank God, somebody showed up!" Yet, Bill Gates is still rich AF, and that's because he's figured out how to monetize all the data on the backend.

If it weren't for Windows, Microsoft would be out of business right now. I've always imagined what it would be like if the Apple store and the Microsoft store were right next door to each other. Microsoft is a third of the price. They have some okay products. But if that were the situation, you know Microsoft's store would be like a ghost town.

Bill Gates sits on the board of Berkshire Hathaway and is one of their executives. I'm pretty sure he got that title by letting them give him billions of dollars to give away to charity. It's almost like it's an Illuminati way of laundering money.

Warren Buffett talked about buying Nebraska Furniture in the 80s, then buying all the trains and railroads. When they did this, they could transfer their furniture because they had control of the railroads. From the railroads, the furniture had to be loaded onto a semi, which led them to buy the fifth largest freight brokerage in America. After that, they bought the largest auto dealer in the world. So, now they control vehicle sales and people who buy cars and houses. But the people who buy houses also buy cars, and the people who buy houses, of course, buy furniture. They're turning into a global Amazon.

Here's another example on the lesson of the importance of data.

Mark Zuckerberg built the website that two billion people use. Now Instagram has a billion users and is the fastest growing site in the history of the world.

When they started with their IPO—their initial public offering—they said Facebook was worth $200B. But to get that valuation they had to figure out how to monetize all the free accounts. Enter selling ads.

If Bill Gates, Warren Buffet, Jeff Bezos and Mark Zuckerberg, the four wealthiest people on the planet made their money from monetizing data, don't you think as a business owner, having a database is pretty damn important?

People are buying companies these days, and they're not buying based on projected sales; they're not buying based on past sales; they're buying based on your database.

The reason why I tell you this is because you need to build a database in the event that your industry is taken over. You don't want to go out of business.

This is why I teach people about the importance of establishing and maintaining a database. In our highest-level mastermind, every week our members check in and they tell us how many people they have added their database. We make them add five people per day, so if you don't have a CRM, get one. Every time someone reaches out to you on Facebook, add them to your database. Maybe you have their email address or phone number; take whatever information you do have and add it, and then include their FB link in your database.

Get into the habit of adding people to your database when you have their information. As they give you more information, enter it into the notes section of the database.

I've built a 120,000-person database for Break Free Academy because I know that I will need it if I ever sell BFA.

The buyer will not purchase it based on the content. They will buy it based on the customer information.

Which brings us to funnels and why they are so vital to your business.

Funnels automatically add people to your database, so they make your work even easier and they put people in there that you might never have spoken to.

I'll give you an example.

Let's say you made a post on Facebook. Then you drop a link into a long-form post at the bottom. That prospect will hit your link, and then they will give you the information you have specified they are to give. They will enter their name email, address, mobile phone number, maybe their home address. Whatever other information you need from them and that you have asked for, they will give you. When we say they opt-in, it means that they have agreed to give you their information.

Once they opt-in, they get their gift. And this gift could be anything; it could be a free list of homes; it might be a free consultation or a free e-book. It doesn't matter what it is; in our language, we call it a free report.

Then they take the next action which can be to click on a link that will ultimately take them to your CRM as a lead. That's the whole point of a sales funnel: to take somebody who's unknown and turn them into a lead in your CRM database.

A funnel works because it has a series of web pages attached to it. A prospect will enter through one of the pages and exit on another, after clicking through individual URL links.

You can begin your funnel on Facebook and then lead your prospect to click on another link that will lead to what's called a landing page. The landing page is where you will have your offer.

The best way to write an offer on your landing page is to follow the "how to get X without Y."

X is what they want. Y is what they don't want. So, for example, "how to make a million dollars without having to work." "How to get the home of your dreams and not owe any money on it." "How to get the lowest priced home in Austin without having to get into a bidding war." "How to get X without y" is the easiest way to write an offer that was invented by Ogilvy. It's the most powerful offer in the world.

"How to get millions of customers on Facebook absolutely free." Ask yourself what that insinuates. "How to get a bunch of customers without having to pay money for them." You can use any variation. And this is the best offer format because it covers everything.

Remember to always ask for a mobile phone number because 99.9% of phone calls go unanswered.

But 99% of text messages get checked.

I can text somebody right now, and they may not read it right in the moment, but they can check it at their convenience. Landlines are going to be obsolete before long anyway.

Let's say the offer is a free video of "how to make a million dollars from social media without having to pay for ads."

In exchange for that free video, they'll give us their name email, address and mobile phone number. This information will go right into your CRM. That's the power of a funnel.

A funnel can have as many pages as you want; it can be as simple as you want.

There's a reason people pay us $6,000-$10,000 to build simple funnels. That's because of the value it brings them.

When I teach the Break Free Academy two-day event the purpose is for people to show up and learn. That way when you leave, and Monday comes, you are not intimidated as if you have to do it all. You are already up and running.

That's also why I invented PhoneSites. It's the simplest, fastest software out there to create funnels. You can use it to build your database. Consider this: If you are posting 80% of your content for them and 20% of your content for you, and you're using that 20% to build your database it saves you a shitload of time while it helps your business. Plus, every time somebody hits you up in the DM and they have a question if you already have a funnel it answers that question, and all you have to do is reply to them with the link.

You can tie in whatever CRM you want to with PhoneSites. You can send out automatic emails and texts from Twilio. PhoneSites makes really simple web pages and allows you to string as many of them together as possible. All you have to do is log in on your phone and literally scroll down the page and fill in the blanks. I've set it up, so it will ask for your headline offer. It will ask you your sub-headline. If you want to put extra text on there, or a picture or video, you can do any of that.

We've been trained by people like Russell Brunson and Frank Kern, who are guys I look up to and respect. So, we know what elements you need in your funnel.

You'll be able to create your first funnel in under 10 minutes. Your funnel might be structured like this: You could opt in for the video on Facebook. Then you would put the video on the second page. Your headline could be something as simple as "Here is your free video."

Your funnel doesn't have to be fancy. The idea is to get the money coming in from the sales, to get people to pay attention. We simply are trying to get the prospect in the front door, so they will opt-in.

After your funnel is built, you can start collecting info by dropping the link into the posts that we talked about.

These simple funnels can make you big money (as crazy as that sounds). My database has made me millions.

When you start building your database on autopilot with links going out with emails attached and that allows for auto-follow-up, it changes your life. I'm living proof of this. I can sit down right now in front of the computer and make $50K within the next hour.

I can do the same thing on social media. I just make a post that reads something like: "If you'd like to come to an event, here's your chance. If you opt-in, we'll give you a one-time offer."

At any given moment three percent of the people in your database are ready to buy from you right now. If I have 120K people in my database, 3% is a rather large number of people who can buy right this second. And I think that percentage would go up when I sweeten the pot if I were to offer a book, for example. Especially if I offer them something that's just a couple of hundred bucks versus a few thousand dollars. You can do the same thing. I teach people to do this all the time. If you're not building that database and you don't have software to help you out on the front end—PhoneSites solves that problem. Again, that is exactly why I created it. People needed their funnels to be simplified so they could keep up and cash in. PhoneSites helps you do that.

Let's say you build a funnel that gets 600 leads and that you kill it with the funnel. You can then click share in the dashboard of PhoneSites and send the link to whoever you want to. That person can switch your name for theirs. Boom, you have a brand-new funnel that you know is proven to rake in the sales.

You don't have to have drag and drop and move a bunch of pictures. You don't even need a desktop. Hence the name, PhoneSites.

Imagine going into a room and saying "Here's how you collect a database, and here's how you compete with

Berkshire Hathaway. And, oh, by the way, I do loans, too, so if you need somebody to prequalify your leads, I can help you." How much power do you think that would give you?

Think of how that would change the perspective of the agents who are listening to you when you're not talking about mortgages. Now, you have flipped the switch in their head. Now, they've changed how they think about you. They can see you as a business consultant because you can teach them how to generate their own leads. This is incredibly valuable. It is life changing. It is business changing.

What if you could give them your affiliate link, so you would make 40% off of their sales every single month? If you're a Realtor and you speak at real estate events, you can get paid for the speaking events you're selling them.

What you have learned in this book can easily be your Bible to changing your business exponentially. Implement M3 today. Then nail it and scale it.

About the Author

A BAMF, unafraid to take action, Ryan Stewman, aka the "Hardcore Closer," is a bestselling author, podcaster and blogger. Best known for consulting with Alpha personality types on rapidly growing their sales via the use of powerful advertising and marketing, Ryan is a salesman turned CEO. He has not had a salaried job his entire life. He's mastered the art of super effective communication and has closed more transactions than he has time to count. With his no-BS approach to strategizing and scaling businesses, Ryan has helped high-net-worth performers adjust their business plans resulting in windfall profits.

After gaining prolific social media experience, Ryan decided to teach people from all sales fields and industries how to sell online. In the first year, Break Free Academy (BFA) closed over $150K in gross sales; the second year BFA hit over $300K; in 2016, BFA generated over $2M, and in 2017, BFA grossed $4M+.

His notoriety and savage sales acumen have put him on the pages of the largest media publications on the planet. He contributes to and has been featured in *Forbes, Entrepreneur, Addicted2Success, The Good Men Project, The Lighter Side of Real Estate* and the *Huffington Post* in addition to other top-tier sites.

He states the key to his success is doing the work.

HardcoreCloser.com is an online learning resource for salespeople, selling e-learning products in the advertising, marketing funnel sales and social media arenas and offers personal coaching and live events. Break Free Academy is Hardcore Closer's flagship program and provides every tool needed to market businesses online and crush the competition.

Ryan was born and raised in Texas. He's a doting husband and proud father to three sons. He and his family live in Dallas.

Subscribe to his blog at www.HardcoreCloser.com

Made in the USA
Columbia, SC
27 January 2025